The

Power

of

Mother

by Nancy Temples

Dedication

This book is dedicated to God
for the blessing of children.
Mary, Mother of all, who
inspired me. My wonderful
husband, Brian and my
beautiful girls, Maria and
Samantha.
Thank you for showing me,
The Power of Mother.

The Power of Mother

The Power of a Mother is the
strongest power on earth.

As a mother, you choose the
path for your children.

A Mother's every move and all
of her
choices will
effect the life of her child.
Before you act or speak,
realize this:

Just one slap, will take away a
piece of their soul

Just one negative word, will
tear down their spirit

Just one wrong decision, will
change their life's path

Just one mistrusting adult, will
haunt their minds forever

A life filled with guidance,
will give them a full and happy
soul

A life filled with positive
words, will build a spirit that
will soar to wonderful heights

A life filled with proper
decisions, will let them follow
their dreams

A life filled with trusting
adults, will help them become
trusting adults

Now, you decide. They are your children, gifts from God, for you to guide, love, and cherish.

The next time you go to yell, hit, or neglect, think before you act.

Love your children with all your heart and soul. Give of yourself always, for their sake, and the Lord will bless you and yours forever.

Say good morning, everyday

Let them know

how happy you are to see them

Say I Love You,

I Love You,

I Love You

Kiss them,

Kiss them,

and

Kiss them

Hug them,

Hug them,

and

Hug them

Listen

intently to them,

everyday

Spend time

with them

Teach them

the importance

of a good education

Help them

achieve a

good education

Teach them religion

and

The Power of God's Love

The Power of Mother

Watch over them,

always

Guide them

through their own mistakes

Show them

they are lessons of learning

Give them positive

reinforcement,

always

Say good night,

Every night

In the end, what do you get?

Wonderful children who love
and adore you

Children who will grow up to
know and
understand,

The Power of Mother

The Power of Mother

Additional copies of this book
are available by mail.
Send $12.00 plus $1.50 for tax
and postage to:

Nancy Temples

PO Box 11

Blakeslee, PA 18610

or email

nancy@thepowerofmother.net

check out my website for other great

gift ideas

thepowerofmother.net

Edited By: Samantha Temples

10% of all after tax profits will

be donated for charitable purposes

www.ingramcontent.com/pod-product-compliance
Lightning Source LLC
Chambersburg PA
CBHW021916040426
42447CB00007B/887